Being with Dying

A Practical Approach to Serving Others
Through Times of Illness and Death

by Sarayu

Mata Amritanandamayi Mission Trust
Amritapuri, Kerala, India

Being with Dying *by Sarayu*
A practical approach of serving others at the time of illness
and death

Published by
  Mata Amritanandamayi Mission Trust
  Amritapuri P.O., Kollam 690525 Kerala, India
  Email: inform@amritapuri.org
  Websites: www.amritapuri.org
           www.embracingtheworld

First edition, February 2011
Second edition, 2011
Third edition, 2013

Typesetting and layout by Amrita DTP, Amritapuri

This book is offered at the Lotus Feet
of our most beloved Amma,
the One beyond life and death.

Om mṛtyu-mathanyai namaḥ

Salutations to the Divine Mother
who destroys death.

Table of Contents

Sri Mata Amritanandamayi Devi 7

Foreword 9

Introduction 12

I. The Dying 19
  Serving the Dying as a Spiritual Practice 20
  Healing 33
  Stress 37
  Loss 40
  Differences Between Men and Women 44
  Stages of Loss 54

II. The Visit 61
  Entering the Room 62
  The Big Pink Elephant 66
  The Invisible Patient 69
  Listening 74
  Emotional Vocabulary 78
  Focus on the Patient 83

In the Room   87
Guilt   93
Finishing Business   100
Having an Agenda   105
Do's and Don'ts   110
Making a Connection   113
Signs   117

III. Death   121
The Dying Process   122
Leaving   129
Respecting Cultural Differences   134
Children   140
Care Giving for the Caregiver   144
Importance of Humor   146
Comforting the Grieving   149
There Is No Death   151
Amma's Words on Death   157

IV. Practical Application   165
List of Feeling Words   168

Sri Mata Amritanandamayi Devi

Through Her extraordinary acts of love and self-sacrifice, Sri Mata Amritanandamayi Devi or 'Amma' (Mother) as She is more commonly known, has endeared Herself to millions around the world. Tenderly caressing everyone who comes to Her, holding them close to Her heart in a loving embrace, Amma shares Her boundless love with all—regardless of their beliefs, their status or why they have come to Her. In this simple yet powerful way, Amma is transforming the lives of countless people, helping their hearts to blossom one embrace at a time. In the past thirty-eight years, Amma has physically hugged more than twenty-nine million people from all parts of the world.

Amma's tireless spirit of dedication to uplift others has inspired a vast network of charitable activities, through which people are discovering the deep sense of peace and inner fulfilment that comes from selflessly serving others. She teaches that the divine exists in everything, sentient and insentient. Realizing this truth is the essence of spirituality—the means to end all suffering.

Amma's teachings are universal. Whenever She is asked about Her religion, She replies that Her religion is love. She does not ask anyone to believe in God or to change their faith, but only to inquire into their own real nature and to believe in themselves.

Foreword

When I heard that a small book had been written by Sarayu on how to interact with people who are dying, I was very interested to read it and learn more. I used to consider people like myself—who haven't had much firsthand exposure to death and dying—fortunate. That is, until I began hearing how valuable and precious so many people consider the time they have spent with those in the final stages of life. Time spent with a dying person doesn't need to be fraught with fear and distress, as we may imagine, but can actually be an incredibly beautiful and profound experience that helps us to grow as human beings.

Because I have never been with someone in the final stage of their life, I felt that I would not know what to do or the correct thing to say if I were to suddenly find myself in that sensitive situation. What a relief to discover that there is actually nothing one really has to do or say; simply "being" with them is enough; hence the name of this book, Being With Dying.

Being With Dying doesn't just refer to being in the presence of a dying person. It refers to "being" with the phenomena of dying in its entirety. And, ultimately, that means being at peace with mortality—both our own and that of our loved ones. Change is the nature of life. That which is born must one day die. However, the caterpillar doesn't enter the cocoon to perish, but rather to cast off its bondage and emerge a beautiful butterfly. Similarly, through spiritual understanding, let us emerge from the cocoon of our fear and misconceptions about death and dying and learn to trust the evolutionary life cycle.

When Amma is comforting people who are ill or mourning the loss of a loved one, She doesn't try to give them any deep spiritual teachings. She usually just holds them and, while drying their tears as well as Her own, tells them not to cry. Witnessing this I used to wonder, "Why isn't Amma saying anything else to them?" However, I've come to understand that in such moments, advice doesn't help. Rather, Amma allows Herself to simply be with them, to become one with them. And in sharing their pain in this way, She transmutes it with Her awareness and love.

By embracing each present moment in all its fullness, Amma shows us how to face the wonder of the great unknown and the mystery of our own mortality with courage and faith. I hope those who read this sweet book will imbibe its essence and thereby find and share peace.

— *Swamini Krishnamrita Prana*
Amritapuri Ashram

Introduction

"Children, even if we are not in a position to
help others materially, we can at least give them
a loving smile or a kind word. It doesn't cost us
anything. What is needed is a compassionate
heart—this is the first step in spiritual life. Those
who are kind and loving towards others have no
need to wander in search of God, because God
will come rushing towards the heart that beats
with compassion. Such a heart is God's favorite
place to live."

—Amma

My father died of cancer when I was twenty-six. At the time of his diagnosis I had been living in Amritapuri for three years. I can still remember receiving that surreal phone call from him, explaining that doctors had found two masses in his lungs. In a confused and shocked state, I went to Amma. She told me to go and be with him immediately. I suddenly found myself being his primary caretaker for the last six months of his life. He was fifty years old when he died.

We had always had a good relationship but the connection that was created through these circumstances was profound and sacred. The love that was always there between us was now openly expressed. This experience impacted me very deeply. The memory of that time with my father is a precious jewel I carry in my heart.

What I didn't realize then, was that by Her simple instruction to go and be with him, Amma was planting a seed. A seed that later was my inspiration to become a chaplain. I served as a chaplain in America between 2003-2005. At this time I had the opportunity to be with people suffering from many different diseases.

During those two years, I was pushed to my limit in a variety of ways. I had to rely strongly on my faith in order to accept, make sense of, or "hold" the amount of suffering I was witnessing. This experience changed me forever.

I worked with people who were deprived of so many of the things we take for granted in life. Some suffered without any resources at all: no loving friends or family to visit them, no strong faith to support them, nor an advocate to help them navigate the health care system.

By being a witness to their needs and suffering, I was shown over and over again what the most important things in life are: to be of service, to pay attention and to love—the more we look at ways to serve the dying, the more we see that the same rules apply for serving the living.

Upon reflection, I realized that this work went hand-in-hand with Amma's teachings and the sadhana (spiritual practices) She recommends. Amma is the perfect chaplain and the pinnacle example for us in all the situations we face in life.

I am not an expert. I have simply tried to pay attention to what was going on around and inside me. I am sharing my experiences, as well as my mistakes, in the hopes that we all deepen our understanding and our ability to be present and care for each other in times of need.

It's quite possible that you will get a similar phone call and someone you know will be diagnosed with a terminal disease. How will you react to this? Do you feel prepared to be with a dying person? What would be the most helpful attitude with which to approach this situation? How can we best serve people who are dying?

Although this book is short, there is a lot of information that may be new to you, so I invite you to read it slowly and take time after each section to reflect, digest, and absorb the ideas, and see how they apply to your own situation.

The Dying

"Sensitive people endowed with compassionate hearts are hard to find. Find your own inner harmony, the beautiful song of life and love within. Go out and serve the suffering. Learn to put others before yourself. Consider everyone, because that is the doorway to God and to your own Self."

—*Amma*

Serving the Dying as a Spiritual Practice

"Many people do not want to meditate because the stillness experienced in meditation makes them think that they are going to die. You do not realize that meditation is the saving principle—that it makes you immortal. Meditation takes you across the cycle of death and rebirth. It actually prevents the fear of death. Spiritual practices give you the power and courage to smile at death."

—*Amma*

The act of sitting with the dying is a tremendously powerful spiritual practice. It is an occasion that calls upon us to put into practice all the qualities that we are striving for in spiritual life: equanimity, compassion, surrender, faith and putting others first. It offers a great opportunity to live Amma's teachings.

In this chapter we will look at some of Amma's spiritual teachings that we can practice while serving a dying person: being in the present moment, accessing patience, remembering the truth that we are not the body but the Self, and opening the heart.

Being in the Present

"Just as a child lives fully in the present, when you love, let your whole being be present in that love, without any divisions or reservations. Don't do anything partially, do it fully by being in the present moment. Don't brood on the past,

and don't cling to it. Forget the past and stop dreaming about the future. Express yourself by being fully present, right now. Nothing, neither the regrets of the past nor the anxieties about the future, should interfere with the flow as you express your inner feelings. Let go of everything, and let your whole being flow through your mood."

—Amma

The most important gift that we can offer to someone who is dying is to be present: to listen actively and give our full attention to that person. Being present means having a heightened awareness and sensitivity to his or her situation, and accepting that person in every changing moment. In this way, the time we spend with the person becomes a form of meditation. Watching Amma give darshan (traditionally, this means seeing a saint, but in this case it means Amma blessing people by hugging them), we witness the power of Her being totally present with another person. One after another, people come to Amma. Some are coming for the first time, some are sad, some are happy, and some are shy. Nonetheless, Amma meets everyone where they are in that moment.

If you are on a spiritual path, trying to learn more about your own fears and unconscious behavior, then you will gain much insight about yourself by sitting with a dying person. If you are used to sitting with or observing your own uncomfortable feelings and thoughts in times of contemplation or meditation, then you will be better equipped for the uncomfortable feelings that arise when sitting with the dying. In fact, any practice—be it meditation, chanting, saying the rosary, going to a 12-step program—will be of great assistance to you and the person you are visiting. Such practices help us remain calm, centered and present—all essential qualities that assist us to serve the dying.

Amma says: "Only a person who leads a moment-to-moment life can be completely free from fear. He alone can embrace death peacefully. This moment-to-moment living is possible only through meditation and doing spiritual practices. When there is ego, there is fear of death. Once the ego is transcended, one becomes egoless and the fear of death also disappears. In that state, death becomes a great moment of celebration."

Patience

"Patience and self-surrender are essential for an aspirant."

—*Amma*

How patient, tolerant and compassionate are we? We will quickly find out when sitting with a dying person on a regular basis. Often our loved ones, previously filled with vigor, begin thinking and moving more slowly. Activities like eating and bathing can take twice as long as they once did. People may even go through significant mood swings and personality changes. These are all situations that test our patience while serving the dying. We need to be vigilant in maintaining patience, because impatience can often lead us to unintentionally impose our will upon others.

The purpose of our spiritual practice is to ultimately be of great benefit to the world. Amma says, "Children, patience is needed to make spiritual progress. Never lose patience. Do your spiritual practices with utmost sincerity and wait patiently. If you are sincere, the results will come."

In the day-to-day experience of serving the ill or dying person, we may find ourselves wanting to rush them through an activity or wishing they would hurry up and make a decision. Amma gives us very practical advice in this regard: "Impatience destroys. Be patient. Real life is love. When you love, you cannot rush. You must be patient. When you are in the midst of an upsetting situation, simply observe what is happening. Don't be abusive. Don't react. Try to realize that the real problem is not what is happening, but how you are reacting to it. When you see that you are going to react negatively, at this point, pause. Stop talking."

Remembering That We are Not the Body but the Self

"If we want mental peace, we should understand the difference between the permanent and the transitory, and act accordingly. All our relatives will depart some day and we will be alone. Therefore, we should think about the real goal of life. If we live with that understanding, we will not even fear death...

It is good if spiritual people visit hospitals at least once a month. This will help make the mind stronger and softer as well. Increasing one's dispassion will give more determination to the mind. The heart will become soft due to compassion... We will understand how silly this life is if we realize that we are next. To really have the awareness that we will die will help increase detachment. Death follows us like a shadow. Knowing and understanding the inevitability of death, one should strive hard to realize the eternal truth before the body falls off. Nobody knows who is next. Nobody can predict it."

—Amma

This work is not for the fainthearted. Sitting with a dying person can be difficult. We are unavoidably confronted with our own mortality. We will find ourselves wondering: How will I die? Who will be there to be by my side? What will it feel like? In times of solitude, we can contemplate and come to grips with our own death. When have we felt the most contentment, peace or joy in our lives? Who and what is really most important to us? Where in our life do we have unfinished business?

Amma tells us, "Remember, at each and every moment, this great threat of death is present. When we realize that, it is a blow to our ego. If we can feel the imminence of death, it will help us to live in the present. It will help us to be concerned about others."

Opening the Heart

"The essence of motherhood is not restricted to women who have given birth; it is a principle inherent in both women and men. It is an attitude of the mind. It is love—and that love is the very breath of life."

—*Amma*

Whether we are male or female, the inner universal Motherhood in all of us gets a chance to blossom when we serve the dying. This experience provides us a beautiful opportunity to get out of our heads and drop into our hearts.

One of Amma's *brahmacharinis* worked as a hospice volunteer in San Francisco before meeting Amma. There she visited a few times with a young woman dying of lung cancer. This woman was difficult to deal with as she was very rude and aggressive.

One day the hospital called the volunteer to tell her that the woman had taken a sudden turn for the worse and would probably die within the next twenty-four hours. They were concerned because they couldn't locate her family. They asked her to come and sit with the patient.

She went to the hospital and as soon as she entered the room, she could see that the young woman was terribly afraid and she was having difficulty breathing. She tried to talk to her, but there was nothing she could say or do to calm her down. So she just sat there for hours. She focused on simply being there with the dying woman, with all her heart and soul. She tried to allow her own heart to be open to the woman's presence and her fear. Eventually the woman seemed to calm down.

After several hours, the woman's family arrived and the hospice worker left the hospital. As she waited for a bus, she felt that her heart was wide open in a way she had never previously experienced before. She felt in the most profound way that she loved everyone and everything. As she boarded the bus, she found that she even wanted to hug the bus driver!

The moments spent with the dying have a different quality to them; all the social masks go out the window. While talking to a dying person we can become more aware of time and the fact that their time is limited. We start to understand that much of what we talk about is actually very insignificant and rarely important. We feel that sense of urgency regarding time and how precious it is, and we gain a deeper understanding of Amma's teaching, "Don't waste time. Amma does not worry about the loss of ten million rupees, but Amma is really concerned about wasting even a single moment. Money can be regained; time that is lost cannot. Children, always be aware of the value of time."

If you spend a lot of time with a dying person, the level of intimacy experienced between you can be very deep. The usual day-to-day 'busyness', the laundry list of things to do, the disagreements with co-workers and all the things that distract us from the present moment are absent a large part of the time when we are visiting our loved one.

We actually may start to realize that the happenings in our life that we call problems are nothing compared to the dying person's situation. This is a gift the dying person unknowingly gives to us. They slow us down and show us what is important and meaningful in life. We can all benefit from this kind of relating to one another on a deeper level. Usually we feel very nourished whenever that heart-to-heart connection happens with others. This is a valuable experience that can enrich us and then we, in turn, can share that experience in other areas of our lives.

Healing

"Love can heal wounded hearts and transform human minds. Through love one can overcome all obstacles. Love can help us renounce all physical, mental and intellectual tension and thereby bring peace and happiness. Love is the ambrosia that adds beauty and charm to life. Love can create another world in which you are immortal and deathless."

—Amma

This process is a cycle: spiritual practice helps us to sit with a dying person, and sitting with a dying person is a tremendously powerful spiritual practice.

It is also a reciprocal process. One's unresolved emotional wounds may be revealed, which can instigate an opportunity for healing. A hospital chaplain told me the following story:

"I was asked to visit a teenage boy who had been shot. He was in critical condition and was not expected to live. When I was told about him, my heart began to beat quickly, and I went to the unit. I don't remember anyone else being in the room—just this unconscious boy with tubes and wires and lights surrounding him. I vaguely recall looking at him for a few minutes, listening to his labored breathing, and then leaving the room. I didn't realize until I was halfway down the corridor that I was holding onto the wall.

My sister was shot in the back of the head when she was sixteen years old. She went into a coma for two days and then died. The bullet that hit my sister shattered our whole family.

We had no belief system, nothing to help us explain this, nothing to hold onto, not even each other. My father did not believe in counseling, saying it was for weak or crazy people. So, we each withdrew into our own confusion and anguish for the next twenty-five years. I was ten years old at the time.

When I was called to the bedside of that boy, who was the same age as my sister when she was shot, I realized I had still not fully healed all the deep wounds I carried from her sudden death, even though I had been working with this issue for many years. I was completely unable to cope with this boy."

Serving a dying person is a very helpful gauge to see where we truly are in terms of emotional maturity. First, we must determine if we are ready and able to cope with the presented situation. If we believe we are unable to help emotionally, we need to make a choice: either to be honest about our incapacity to participate or, to be willing to see it as an opportunity to begin or deepen our self-healing process. The important factor is that we remain aware of how we are affected by the circumstances. Elisabeth Kübler-Ross[1], in her seminal work on hospice care, *Living with Death and Dying*, explains, "It is essential that everyone caring for the dying and their families understands at all times their own concerns and anxieties in order to avoid a projection of their own fears."[2]

---

[1] Elisabeth Kübler-Ross, M.D. (1926 – 2004) was a Swiss-born psychiatrist and the author of the groundbreaking book *On Death and Dying*. Her dedication and determination forever changed how the world treats its dying. Her tireless efforts to assure that those who are dying be treated with compassion and dignity have now become the standard in end of life care. Dr. Ross taught the world that dying was actually about living and that our work here was to learn how to love unconditionally.

[2] Kübler-Ross, Elisabeth. *Living with Death and Dying*. New York: Macmillan, 1981, page 16.

Stress

It's important to remember that sickness and death are extremely stressful. Many of the events that are happening are unpredictable and unfamiliar. We usually associate stress with activity. Thus, if someone is lying in bed, we do not recognize it as stressful. For most people, stress usually brings out their worst side—this is true, not only for the dying, but also for caregivers and loved ones. Looking at it in this light and asking ourselves, "What helps me to cope with stress?" will be very helpful, especially if we can incorporate those coping skills into our daily lives.

However, not everyone responds to illness with stress. Some people slow down because of illness, and begin to appreciate many things about their lives. They discover the chance to experience a tremendous amount of gratitude toward the people and things in their lives that make them happy. So, as with most life experiences, it is important to consider that many different reactions can occur.

Often, at some point during the process of being with someone through a critical illness, we feel a sense of powerlessness and loss of control. No matter how much we want things to be different, no matter how much we love the person, we cannot change what they are going through. It is normal to feel helpless and powerless at times; in fact, we are powerless. Learning to accept our powerlessness and to surrender control becomes a necessary step toward spiritual maturity. Ideally, we want to learn how to surrender gracefully and with the proper understanding—a process which could be called accepting how life unfolds as God's Will, or faith in a higher power.

Many illnesses are degenerative, causing the body to slowly and gradually deteriorate over the course of years. These progressive diseases are very painful, and patients usually require long term care. The issues discussed in this book—stress, loss, hope, etc—apply not only when our loved ones are diagnosed with a terminal disease, but also when they are diagnosed with chronic illnesses.

When caring for someone who is severely ill or dying, it's normal for a caregiver or friend to feel stress, exhaustion, confusion, upset or sadness. Be tolerant with yourself; your caring and presence are priceless gifts.

Loss

"*Spiritual realization is the ability to hold a caring attitude towards all beings, to look through the third eye while keeping your other two eyes wide open. The fulfilment of spirituality is the ability to accept and understand others as they are.*"

—*Amma*

The terminally ill patient faces the most vulnerable situation of his or her entire life. There are many things we need to consider in order to be more sensitive to exactly what is happening for the person who is facing illness and death.

In death, this being we call "I" loses everything. You may be losing someone you love very much, but the person who is dying is losing everyone they love and everything they love. The experience of loss begins at the time of diagnosis. Everything changes, especially the person's relationship to their body and how it works. It is even common to feel betrayed by one's own body.

As soon as a person enters a hospital, a huge change is already taking place in their life. When we are visiting the dying, we need to be aware of this. Healthy people live in their homes, where they are comfortable. They eat the food they want to eat when they want to eat it. They have choices. They play different roles throughout the day and they receive attention. They interact with people on all different levels. They experience physical intimacy with their spouse or partner. They spend their free time as they wish.

When someone enters a hospital, they suddenly find themselves in what is usually a very uncomfortable bed with scratchy sheets—having to stare at bad artwork on the walls for ten hours a day. The hospital robe does not fit properly, exposing the patient's backside. No one knocks before entering the room or asks if it is a good time for a visit. Nurses and doctors and cleaners and food servers enter the room all day and night. The patient is not only separated from family and loved ones, but also has no privacy whatsoever.

Another huge change for the patient is that their body is no longer their own. People probe and poke it, cause it pain, expose it and stare at it. The body is intruded upon in ways no one would ever think to touch or regard it outside of the context of the illness. The body becomes an object to examine and cure. The person inside can be forgotten.

How people see themselves, and thus how they experience the world, changes with illness. This body, with which we are so identified, no longer looks, feels or moves the same way. People may experience hair loss, weight loss or even the loss of an organ or limb. If their identity is based upon their physical appearance, such changes can cause a tremendous amount of grief and fear.

A terminal diagnosis immediately changes every relationship one has with others. People no longer relate to the dying person in the same way. Talking openly and honestly and comfortably—especially arguing or disagreeing—are things of the past. Participation in life is dramatically reduced. Added to this is the decision-making process about possible treatments and the side effects that go along with them. Then there is the enormous fear of the unknown—the terrifying thought that their life might never return to its previous, healthy state.

Thus, a person can go overnight from having a very full and active life to being very isolated, frightened and lonely. Keeping this in mind will help us to be more sensitive and empathetic toward our loved one.

Differences Between
Men and Women

"Women and men are not two, but one. They are two aspects of the one truth—like two sides of a coin. What women cannot do, men can. What men cannot do, women can. Their dharmas (duties) are complementary."

—Amma

Because women and men sometimes walk through life in very different ways, the issues that can come up for them with a terminal illness may also vary. I have no wish to stereotype men and women. I include this topic because this disparity was so prevalent in my experience with sick and dying people.

When I first began visiting patients I was not at all aware of these differences. After a couple of months of doing this work, however, I was amazed to see a pattern in almost all of my patients.

For example, when diagnosed with cancer, women generally change roles from being caregivers to people who must ask for and receive help. Many women are not used to asking for help. As such, they feel that by expressing their needs, they are being a burden to their loved ones. Men generally feel very distressed because they can no longer work and support their family.

When I became more aware of these common themes that can occur for men and women, I was able to be sensitive to their situations and, as a result, my visits became more meaningful.

The following is an example of a conversation between a visitor and a female patient. This dialogue offers us a glimpse into some of the issues women typically face: changing roles, asking for help, being a burden to the family, protecting the spouse, and missing loved ones. This is not a formula. There are no perfect questions or responses.

Dialogue No. 1 - Changing of Roles (Female Patient).

Visitor: How are you?

[Patient immediately begins to cry. Visitor allows her to cry for awhile. The patient eventually asks for a washcloth, which the visitor provides.]

Visitor: Do you know where your tears are coming from?

Patient: Yes. I think I'm overwhelmed, I guess. I'm so lucky. The surgery went perfectly. But, my husband and family... *[starts to cry harder]*.

It's been so hard on them. My husband is having a really hard time. He has to take care of the kids and still go to work. I know he is worried about money.

Visitor: I can see by your tears that this has been a really difficult time for you. Sounds like a change of roles for both of you. You must miss being there to take care of everybody.

Patient: Yes. I feel like I can cry with you because you are safe. I can't let him see me lose it. It would add to the stress.

We can see that the visitor responds to what is happening in the moment—allowing the patient to voice her fears and emotions. The issues raised are very powerful and clearly important in this person's life: money, family, stress, physical illness and dependence on others.

The next dialogue addresses some issues that are more common among men.

Dialogue No. 2 - Provider Issues (Male Patient)

Visitor: How has your life changed since you first were diagnosed four months ago?

Patient: Well, when I got really sick, I had to stop working. My wife, Claire, was with me here through everything. So now she has to work a lot.

Visitor: Are you alone a lot now?

Patient: Yes, I am.

Visitor: How is that for you?

Patient: A little hard. With the business, you know, I can't lift anything.

Visitor: You miss the work.

Patient: Yeah, I don't know what to do now.

Visitor: I guess it's pretty isolating for you.

Patient: Yeah, you're right, it is.

Visitor: How is it for you that Claire has to work so hard now?

Patient: It's tough. I feel envious.

Having to rely on his wife for income and feeling helpless and weak challenges this patient's concept of himself, which creates stress on top of coping with his illness. This patient does not feel guilty that his wife has to work more—he feels envious. Men more commonly fill the provider role in the household, and can become identified with the job that they do outside the home. When they cannot work because of illness, they no longer recognize themselves, and sometimes feel useless. These profound emotions often lead to depression. While men generally share this experience, women may also have similar emotions and responses to their changed role in the household.

Developing awareness of these issues better prepares us for our visits, and for whatever emotions the person might experience. Here is another dialogue with a male patient that deals with these exact issues, as well as the issue of wanting to die.

Dialogue No. 3 - Provider Issues (Male Patient)

Visitor: Hi, John. How are you?

Patient: Fine.

Visitor: Are you in here for some treatment?

Patient: I'm getting radiation. I asked the doctor if I could just go and he said, "No."

Visitor: You want to go home?

Patient: No, I want to get buried.

Visitor: You have had enough?

Patient: Yes, I hate just laying in this bed. For the past fifteen months, I've been sick—first in the lung and now in the brain. Even at home I have to stay in bed. My two sons are here from Arizona. I told them to go home.

Visitor: Sounds like you are in a very difficult situation.

Patient: Yeah, I just want to go to sleep, get an injection and go to sleep. But my wife, she says, "No."

Visitor: Do you feel conflicted because she disagrees with you?

Patient: A little. She believes God takes you when He is ready.

Visitor: And you feel differently?

Patient: Well, no. I just want to sleep. There is no purpose for me to lie around like this just watching everyone else walk by, and I can't walk.

Visitor: Do you feel useless because you are not being productive?

Patient: I worked my whole life; I travelled all over the country... I don't know.

Visitor: It sounds like you were very active and now everything has changed.

[Silence]

Visitor: Do you feel at peace with dying?

Patient: *[Hesitates.]* Yeah, but my wife isn't ready. She thinks I have to wait to be called. I'm just tired of all this.

Sometimes the patient feels ready and wants to die, perhaps because of severe chronic pain, or as in this dialogue, because he feels useless. Family members and friends may feel differently, and this conflict often creates a feeling of separation or aloneness for the patient. These feelings may be intensified by the presence of the medical staff, all of whom are diligently working to keep the patient alive. In such cases, we need to be sensitive to this person's feelings.

If we also have a hard time supporting the patient in respect to this issue, we may process those feelings and emotions with a friend or therapist.

Stages of Loss

Elisabeth Kübler-Ross' stages of grief are a very well-known part of the dying process: Anger, denial, bargaining, depression, and acceptance.[3] From the moment of diagnosis, one of the five stages is usually operating in the dying person and their loved ones. I remembered passing through all five stages in a single day.

In my second year as a chaplain, I entered the room of Alex, an eighteen-year-old girl, who was racing against the clock in desperate need of a lung transplant. Immediately we had a connection. I

[3] Ross, *Living With Death and Dying,* back cover.

spent three hours with her, discussing what happens after one dies, if suicide is ever justifiable, her fears, her feelings of isolation, her family, as well as things that every eighteen-year-old goes through (for example, why her boyfriend wasn't calling her). She also shared with me various ways in which she had been coping with her illness. For instance, when she became too tired to keep up with her friends as they walked through the mall, she would make excuses to stop so she could catch her breath, such as, "Oh, look at this shirt! Look at these shoes!"

Her openness with me was remarkable. Needless to say, after three hours I had become attached to her. I was touched by her strength and courage. As she talked, sometimes she would start to cough and become unable to catch her breath—she would start to turn blue. At one point she had to be temporarily put on a respirator. Witnessing this, I felt heartbroken and powerless.

I was very affected emotionally by this visit. On the train home, I began to pray to God. I became aware of many strong feelings that were coming up in me—anger, confusion and sadness. I also felt very depressed and helpless. In trying to find a solution, I began to bargain, even wondering if it could be possible for me to give her one of my lungs. My thoughts stirred on and on.

The whole night I tossed and turned, going through all these stages of grief. The next morning, after meditating for a while, I came to a place of some clarity and acceptance, but not fully. When I went to visit that morning, Alex was not in the room. I thought she had died. Tears sprang to my eyes. I asked the nurse, who told me that she was in surgery. Someone had died, and lungs were brought by helicopter in the middle of the night.

In this situation, I was only an acquaintance, yet you can see how powerfully and fully I experienced the five stages of grief. One can only imagine what the dying person is going through.

These stages can come in any order, and they may last a minute, a day, a month or a year. There is no set formula or pattern. But we should keep in mind that these feelings are natural and normal for the dying person and their loved ones. For example, if you visit a dying friend and find him or her complaining about the food, the nurse's incompetence—even criticizing you—just try to remember that anger is one of the stages, and that this is how your friend's anger is manifesting at this moment. Do not take it personally, and try not to react or become judgmental.

Denial is a very complex state of mind that often plays a role for the dying person or someone very close to them. We sometimes assume it would be healthier if the dying person were to accept and deal with their impending death.

Often the person's denial affects loved ones, usually the children, and the person's unwillingness to accept their own death seems to encourage and prolong denial amongst family and friends. Some people are never ready to talk about their death, and die without ever having discussed it. This does not necessarily mean that they were in denial.

Sometimes people go to great lengths to "protect" their children or spouses. They have the right to decide how they are going to die. Even if we think it seems psychologically unhealthy or repressed, it's not our place to judge—when it is our turn, we can do it the way that we want.

Occasionally people are in denial for what seems like a very long time when they hear that their spouse or child is terminally ill. We may be tempted to bring them into our version of reality. It can really test one's patience to sit and listen to someone who refuses to believe their loved one is sick, especially if the denial lasts for days, weeks or even months.

The kind of support to offer at this time should not be goal-oriented. It is not a problem to be solved. If we are problem-solvers by nature, we need to adjust our way of thinking and realize that what is needed now is more about being and less about doing. Simply being present with another person's confusion and pain is most helpful to them.

The underlying truth, which is often overlooked, is that no one really knows when someone is going to die. We may think that someone is in denial, but he or she may just be in the state of "not knowing," which is actually closer to the truth. People go into remission, miracles can happen or an illness might go on for years. We can never know for sure, even if it looks like the patient is going to die very soon.

My friend related the following story to me:

"I had a friend whose father was in the hospital, and they thought he was going to die. But her mother ended up having a sudden heart attack, out of the blue, and died almost immediately, while her father recovered."

The Visit

"*People want to live forever. No one wants to die. The thought that after your death the world will continue without you makes you tremble. The world will go on without you, and you are going to miss everything that is beautiful: your house, your friends, your wife, your children, the flowers in the garden and their fragrance. Because death is the greatest threat, the greatest fear, the greatest blow to our ego, each moment human beings try to cover up and forget this fear of death by running after pleasures of the world.*"

—*Amma*

Entering the Room

Imagine that we are on our way to visit a person who has been diagnosed with a serious illness. Before we walk into the room, we take a couple of deep breaths and center ourselves.

When visiting the sick and dying, two hearts connect, and a sacred space opens up. It is most helpful if we participate in a grounded, sensitive and open mood. In this atmosphere, we have the opportunity to learn many things about ourselves; the dying patient often serves as a mirror that reflects back our own fear of loss, sadness, negativity and control issues. We then can look closely at our reactions and ask ourselves, "What happened that made me want to run screaming out of that room?"

It has been said that ninety-three percent of all communication is non-verbal. How we enter a room, how we sit and how we relate to the person is actually more important than what we say. What kind of message are we conveying if we sit eight feet away, across the room, in the chair closest to the door? What does it tell the person if we cannot make eye contact, if we simply continue to look out the window?

Even if the person is just an acquaintance, don't be afraid to pull the chair right up next to the bed. If you feel comfortable, and it is not a problem (for example, there is not an IV attached) gently touch his or her hand. Most people in the hospital are not touched in a loving manner. They get poked and prodded and examined, but not held or caressed.

The manner in which Amma chooses to give darshan shows us how important touch is. In the interest of keeping Amma's body healthy, many devotees have begged Amma to change Her approach and merely tap people on the head to bless them, but Amma refuses even at the cost of Her own comfort. She knows that being held closely has a lasting and transformative impact on everyone who experiences Her powerful embrace.

We never want to underestimate the nurturing and healing power of our own touch, especially when working with people who are dying. In a very simple way we can ask the patient, "Is it OK if I hold your hand?" or "Would you like a foot rub?"

At some point during our visit or visits, we will probably feel the urge to do something for the person we are visiting. This impulse is totally natural and normal. There are little things that one can do to make the patient more comfortable. Of course we want to ask before doing anything, but here are some suggestions: propping the pillows, giving a sip of water (if appropriate—you may have to check with the nurse) or administering oral care, like wetting the lips with a sponge, reading to the person, giving them a cold cloth for their forehead, etc.

If the patient is at home receiving hospice care, we might want to help the caregiver by bringing over a meal or doing some simple task like cleaning the dishes. We can also ask the primary caretaker what they might need. Such little actions will help us feel useful and can be greatly appreciated.

The Big Pink Elephant

When we visit a dying person we may think there are only two people in the room—you and the dying person. But, in fact, there is a third presence—'the big pink elephant.' Many times I have witnessed friends and family members during their first visit to a sick friend or relative. They talk about the weather, current news and sports, and never address the big pink elephant—the reason why the person is hospitalized. Don't be afraid to voice it.

Here are some possible things we could say. "Dad, we have never talked about death. What are some of the beliefs you have around death?" Or

"Mary, what kinds of thoughts and feelings have you been having since your diagnosis?" If this seems too confrontational, we can simply pull up a chair, look the person in the eye and say, "How are you doing with all of this?" This simple statement lets the person know that we are willing to go to a place with them that could be emotionally difficult. If the person, in turn, answers us by talking about the weather, that is fine—that is their prerogative. Maybe tomorrow the person will remember that we are willing to talk about feelings and emotions. At least we have opened the door.

The dying person also might test us to see how much courage we have and if we really are someone who can be trusted with their feelings. This can sometimes look like the patient is angry and very hostile towards us—maybe blaming us for their situation, for example, for putting them in the hospital. I had this experience, and after I came back the next day for a visit, the patient said to me, "So I didn't scare you away after all. I was sure you wouldn't come back."

Sometimes we may feel at a loss, unable to imagine what the person is experiencing. In such cases, it may be helpful to establish an open dialogue to voice those feelings, and say, "I just can't imagine what you are going through right now. Can you describe it to me?"

The Invisible Patient

"Though an object is right in front of us, if our mind is not there, we will not see it. It is said, 'It is not enough that you have eyes, you need to see.'"

—*Amma*

Sometimes I have the feeling that patients want to scream, "Look at me! Listen to me! Understand me!" I have seen many doctors, nurses, food servers, etc, practically ignore the patient. Possibly, this happens because it is very hard for anyone to watch another person in pain. Of course, if they are our loved one, it is even more difficult, and this is one of the most challenging situations for us to be in. If we find ourselves ignoring the person because we feel scared or uncomfortable, we can immediately check ourselves and turn our attention back to him or her. We can even say, "Sometimes it is so hard for me to watch when you are in pain."

After most of my visits, I felt aware of the feelings of isolation and loneliness that are a part of so many patients' experiences. Some family members just can't "be there" for them emotionally, or as we have just discussed, patients become invisible—not listened to, and not seen by the medical staff caring for them.

Once I was visiting Brian, a teenage boy who was completely paralyzed due to a motorbike accident. He was about to go into surgery, and his parents were also in the room. The nurse came in and spoke only to his mother, literally speaking over his reclining body to do so. After she left the room, Brian said to his mother, "Next time a nurse comes in, I want them to talk to me directly. Will you help me with this?" This was a great example of clear, straightforward communication and asking for help.

I only spent about one hour with Brian, but we made a very deep connection. I empathized with him because I also suffered from a car accident when I was young. I was paralyzed for a time and had to undergo a very serious surgery.

When I got the call to visit this boy, my shift in the hospital had just ended and I was on my way out the door. The phone rang and, for some reason, I turned back and answered it. The nurse said she didn't really know why she was calling me, but she felt this boy needed to talk to someone. After I met her and she explained his situation, I told her that I had also been in an accident fifteen years prior, after which I had been paralyzed and had surgery. She started to cry because of the "coincidence", but I knew an unseen hand was guiding me to this boy because I could empathize with his situation.

Normally, it is better not to talk about ourselves while visiting someone who is in need of our care and attention. However, if we have had a similar experience, it can be beneficial to simply and briefly voice it at the outset. You will be amazed at the change in the other person from relating to them in this way. Brian suddenly looked at me like I was the only one who truly had understood him throughout his ordeal.

If you find yourself in a similar situation, it is important not to dismiss the patient's fears, or placate them with empty words like, "You will be fine, just like me." Remember what it was like for you—scary or lonely, etc—when you were going through your difficult situation. Listen and continue to support them in each moment.

With this kind of presence, patients will feel understood and supported when they are reminded that they are not the only ones who have undergone this experience.

In general, if you have suffered physically or emotionally in your own life, you will have greater empathy and compassion for others. We bring our own experiences to the bedside, and it is the hard times, the times in which we suffered, that prepare us to sit with people who are frightened or in pain.

Amma tells us, "Only a person who has known hunger will understand the pangs of hunger in another person. Only a person who has carried a heavy load will understand the strain of carrying heavy weights. If each of us really wanted to, we could make a big difference in the world. The benefit of all the good actions that we perform with a selfless attitude will definitely come back to us."

Listening

"Real listening happens only where there is love."
—*Amma*

If we are tired of talking about the weather and the news, and want to go to a deeper level of intimacy but don't know exactly how to start, one or two good questions can take us there. For instance, if a woman has been in the hospital for a long time, we might ask what she misses the most from her "normal" life. Her answer reveals to us exactly where she is in that moment. Her answer might surprise you. We might have thought that she would say her husband or kids, but she very well may say she misses gardening. Another question could be, "What have you learned about yourself these last four months since your diagnosis?" This question can shift the patient from the superficial to a more introspective dialogue without becoming too personal.

Any ordinary subject initiated by a dying person can suddenly take on a deeper significance. For example, a person who previously was an athlete and is now limited by sickness may open a subject related to sports. This may act as an invitation to talk about a loss in their life, not just to hold a superficial conversation. If we are not paying close attention, we could miss this opportunity to connect more deeply.

The desire to help others comes from a very pure place inside each one of us. But ultimately, we cannot help anyone face death unless we have overcome the fear of death ourselves. And who among us has completely overcome the fear of death? Therefore, the best most of us can do is to simply sit beside someone and try to really hear them, without judgment and without wanting to change his or her process. This is very difficult to do.

Amma explains to us, "There are four ways for improving the exchange of ideas: reading, writing, speaking and listening. Beginning from childhood, we are trained for the first three disciplines. However, we haven't had much training in listening. That is why many of us are poor listeners. Actually, God has given us two ears and one mouth. We need to be ready to listen twice as much as we speak. Right now we do the opposite. We keep speaking and we are not ready to listen."

How we listen to the words of a dying person is very important. We can try to identify the emotions we hear behind the person's words. Then, we can merely reflect the emotion we think we have heard. Once practiced, this technique is actually very simple, and can also be used in our daily lives, whenever someone comes to talk with us about something of importance. We can begin by stopping what we are doing, giving the other person our full attention, listening with our whole being and then reflecting back the emotions we hear. If we understood incorrectly, the person will let us know. We need to be careful not to placate or try to change the feelings that the person may be having in the moment. Our goal is to listen and empower, not to judge. This is a very crucial point.

Emotional Vocabulary

People, whether they are healthy or in the process of dying, want to be heard. The best way to listen is by trying to recognize the emotions behind their words. Many people have a very limited emotional vocabulary; the following is a dialogue with a woman, who is not well-equipped to describe her emotional life.

Dialogue No. 4 - Limited Emotional Vocabulary

Visitor: How are you?

Patient: Well, it's hard.

Visitor: What's hard? *[Visitor smiles at her and touches her arm.]*

Patient: To be away from my family.

Visitor: Are you feeling lonely?

Patient: Yes.

Visitor: How does it feel when you are separated from your family?

Patient: I don't like it.

Visitor: Could you tell me more about that?

Patient: We are a very... close family. We are... upright and... moral.

Visitor: It sounds like you are very proud of your family.

Patient: I am.

Visitor: How does it feel to be away from them?

Patient: Sad.

Visitor: Can you tell me about them?

Patient: Yes. We love each other very much. My children are all... good people. I feel separated from them.

Visitor: Do you think it's because you are in the hospital?

Patient: No, I feel it all the time. It will be... sad when we are not together.

Visitor: Do you mean if someone dies?

Patient: Yes. It's hard when someone dies.

Visitor: Yes, it is. *[Pause]* Are you talking about your own death?

Patient: Yes.

Visitor: What will make your death hard?

Patient: I will leave them... I don't think I can leave them.

Visitor: You miss them very much when you are not with them.

Patient: Yes. We are so close... We love each other.

Visitor: How do you feel when you think about your death? *[Visitor gently strokes her forehead.]*

Patient: Sad.

When the patient has difficulty talking about his or her feelings, it is best to try to avoid using yes/no questions, because these intrinsically do not allow for much elaboration or description, especially if the person has a limited emotional vocabulary. After some time you may start to feel like a newspaper reporter who is simply drilling out one question after another.

While listening to our friend or loved one, we can pay attention to see if they express any needs. These may be practical, immediate needs like a drink of water, or emotional needs like needing a safe environment in which to cry. Throughout this entire process, we can constantly ask ourselves, "Am I able to fulfill any needs that this person has?"

We can also simply reflect back what we hear. Listening without judgment and giving the other person our full attention is all that is expected of us. We are not going to make all of the pain go away, nor are we going to solve all the person's problems. But when we reflect what a person is feeling, we allow them to feel understood. This need to be understood is very deep in us. When this need is met, it brings a feeling of reassurance.

Focus on the Patient

*"Amma has a strong wish that all of her children
will become so pure that they will spread light
and love to whomever they meet. It is not
preachers, but living examples that this world
needs."*

—*Amma*

When we are with a dying person, we never want to
preach or give a sermon, or even talk about our own
belief system. Our spiritual practices and beliefs are
for us—to support and sustain us before and after we
visit the dying person. It is how we will make sense
of or "hold" the suffering.

For example, we avoid saying things like "You're not the body," or "It's all God's grace," "It's your *karma*." to a person who is suffering. When we say something like this, we can almost hear the thoughts of the other person: "Easy for you to say. You're not the one who has to face this."

Though we may share such sentiments, and offer them with the best of intentions, they only add to the patient's feelings of separation. Even if you are both from the same spiritual or religious background, do not make any assumptions. We each have a unique relationship with life; therefore, we each have a different philosophy toward delicate matters such as illness and death.

If someone we are visiting sincerely asks about our faith, we may allow ourselves to openly share our way of living. It is beneficial to then ask the patient to share their beliefs and ways of living. We never know when patients may be interested in hearing different perspectives. In fact, looking for other perspectives and discussing their own views can help them gain clarity regarding the beliefs that will best assist them with their current situation.

During our visits, we want to discuss the here and now, ask the patients how they are doing, feeling, etc. Try to keep the focus on the present situation. We can ask questions like "What is the hardest part of all of this for you?" We do not want to visit someone and start a conversation like, "So! What was it like to grow up in Detroit in the '60s?" The first question addresses the patient's feelings now, in the present. The latter puts the emphasis on the past.

Still, if, for example, a person with cancer opens a conversation by saying, "Oh, for a week now I have been thinking about my Aunt Tilly from Tennessee," that is a different story. We could ask, "What exactly about her are you thinking about?" And perhaps you will come to find out that her aunt had died of cancer. It is very different if the patient opens a new topic that may seem unrelated. We should follow through with whatever subject is raised. Our capacity to listen, in general, changes when we sit with the dying. The quality of our listening becomes more attentive and sincere.

When we look at Amma, and how She helps people, we can see that Her focus is never on Herself. It is always on the person who has come to Her.

In fact, Amma says that, in some regards, She functions as a mirror, reflecting the emotions and mental state of the various people who come for *darshan*.

When people coming to Amma are sad, She reflects that sorrow back to them. When they are happy, She reflects their joy. By understanding and reflecting their emotions, Amma becomes a tremendous support for people. Finally, they feel that someone knows them, someone understands them. People take tremendous comfort and strength from this feeling of being understood.

In the Room

"Children, learn to be relaxed in all circumstances. Whatever you do and wherever you are, relax and you will see how powerful it is. The art of relaxation brings out the power that exists within you; through relaxation you can experience your infinite capacities. It is the art of making your mind still and of focusing all your energy on the work you are doing, whatever it may be. Thus you will be able to bring out all your potential. Once you learn this art, everything happens spontaneously and effortlessly."

—*Amma*

You might wonder why it is important to be aware of the differences between men and women, the changes that occur for a person diagnosed with serious illness, the tendency for a patient to feel angry, etc. The better we understand a situation, the more relaxed we will be. Being in the presence of a relaxed and calm person helps others to be relaxed and calm. Thus, the more relaxed we are, the more relaxed the person we are visiting will feel—this will definitely have a positive effect. One of the reasons we feel such peace in the presence of saints like Amma is due to the level of peace experienced in their minds. The peace of their mind is so powerful that it creates a similar effect upon our mind—not unlike the phenomenon of sympathetic vibration.

How comfortable are you with silence? This question is important because there will be a lot of silent moments when we sit with a dying person. They may be too physically weak to talk, or might be in a more pensive mood than usual.

Many of us, in fact, do most of our talking simply to fill the silence. While experiencing the silent atmosphere of a dying person, we can better understand and see the value in Amma's teachings on silence, "Children, speak less, and only when it is absolutely necessary. When you do say a word, say it very carefully because a seeker or a devotee should not utter meaningless things, even if only a single word."

Taking time to be in solitude will also help us to become more comfortable with silence. It does not mean that we have to go live in a forest. We can practice being silent in a library where there may be people around but no communication or going on a long walk by ourselves—with no cell phone. This will prepare us for our own future as well, for when we are growing old or dealing with illness, our inter-action with the world will become decreased. If we are not used to being alone with our own body and mind, we may feel very lonely, fearful or depressed at a later stage.

We all want to give solutions to people when we hear their problems, even before they ask. Listening patiently, without interrupting, is a great form of self-discipline, an exercise in self-restraint. Our tendency is always to comment, or even worse, compete with them, rushing in to tell them our experience which is bigger or better.

How comfortable are you when another person is crying? Once a friend of mine was sitting with a friend who was dying. The dying woman suddenly began to cry. Instead of just quietly allowing her to cry, she tried to console her and asked, "Why are you crying?" The woman immediately stopped and did not reply. If someone starts to cry in the middle of a conversation, we could say something like, "I can see you have a lot of feelings about that. Do you want to talk about it?" They may not. They may say, "No," and keep crying. That's fine; your job is to quietly sit with them, just to be there with the person.

Don't try to be wise and don't put pressure on yourself to say all the right things. This is impractical. Just show up and keep an open heart. If that is our intention the patient will feel it. Don't look for evidence of your presence to have a profound or positive effect. If you really can't determine what your dying friend or relative needs, try to put yourself in their place and ask yourself, "If this was happening to me, what would I want or need from a friend or visitor right now?"

Hope is a quality that is always changing. Initially, most patients hope the diagnosis proves wrong. Then hope shifts to hoping for successful treatments. Again hope may change to something like "I hope my husband can handle the kids without me." Finally, it could be: "I just hope I go quickly." Instead of assuming that the patient has given up hope, we can simply ask, "What do you hope for today?" This line of inquiry brings us into the present moment. We can then talk about today's hopes, bridging from "big picture hope" to "in-the-moment-hope."

We can also view hope in another context. People who are suffering from an illness, especially over a long period of time, sometimes struggle to keep their spirits up. Depression can very slowly and insidiously creep in and affect their day-to-day life. We may not realize that our visits may help them to feel a part of life and on a subtle level inspire hope—at least for today.

Guilt

"*Don't react to the past. There is force and aggression implied in reaction. Reaction creates more turbulence in the mind and the very thought you are trying to forget will come up with much more strength. To react is to fight. Fighting the wounds of the past will only deepen those wounds. Relaxation is the method that heals the wounds of the mind, not reaction.*"

"*The mere realization of your wrongdoing has freed you from it. You have already been forgiven. The pain you have suffered is more than enough to wash away the sin. Any sin will be washed away by the tears of repentance... From now on*

you shouldn't carry this burden in your mind.
Forget it and be at peace".

—*Amma*

When people are seriously ill they have a lot of time
to think about the past. Sometimes guilt or regret
comes up for people who are facing death. They
may need to voice their regrets and even confess
some wrong doing or divulge a secret they have been
carrying for a long time. Usually the patient simply
just wants someone to hear them and bear witness
to their story. If, for example, someone feels guilty
about having done something twenty years ago for
which they now feel regret, we might ask, "At the
time, under the circumstances, were you doing your
best to cope?" And usually people realize that yes,
they were doing their best. This realization helps
them to forgive themselves. At this time we try to
listen with an open heart to what may be quite painful for the patient.

Faith issues also commonly arise when faced with a terminal illness. Many people almost immediately wonder what they have done wrong to deserve this illness or if God is angry with them. If someone asks us something like, "Why is God punishing me?" we could start a dialogue by asking, "Can you tell me more about your relationship with God?"

As portrayed in the following dialogue, guilt can express itself in a number of ways. The person who is dying may feel their relationship with God is being tested, they may feel they cannot speak freely in front of their caregiver, or that they are burdening their loved ones.

Dialogue No. 5 - Guilt and Faith Issues

Visitor: Hi.

Patient: *[to husband]* Bob, will you go out for a while so we can talk?

Visitor: How are you, Rosa?

Patient: Well, I've had three surgeries now. It's been really tough. I've felt like giving up at times. I've really prayed. At times I've lost my faith. Now I seem to be doing better and I feel bad that I didn't believe that God was with me or listening to me.

Visitor: During those hard times, did you feel discouraged and even angry at God?

Patient: Yes. *[pause]* I could never say this to my mother! She has so much faith. She is always saying, "God takes care of everything."

Visitor: And sometimes that doesn't feel true for you?

Patient: Right. *[pause]* She has perfect faith.

Visitor: What does perfect faith look like?

Patient: Hmmm… I guess one who never worries, who is totally accepting of whatever happens to them. *[laughs]* You're right; I guess no one really has perfect faith.

[Long pause. The two sit in silence. A sadness comes over the patient's face.]

Visitor: Do you feel sad right now?

Patient: *[bursts into tears]* Yes.

Visitor: *[after a short time]* What are you feeling sad about?

Patient: My family, the kids, Bob… I feel so bad that they have to go through this. They worry so much, and they are calling all the time. And he is such a good husband. No one could ever have a husband like him. He never complains. None of them do. They are all so wonderful.

Visitor: Do you feel like you are burdening them?

Patient: Yes. Normally I am the one who always looks after everybody else.

Visitor: Sounds like there has been a change in roles and you are not comfortable with that.

Patient: Yes, that's it.

Visitor: Is it hard for you to ask for help?

Patient: Yes. I never had to before this. You remember, I had to help take care of my mother. I know it can be hard sometimes.

Visitor: And you want to spare your family this?

Patient: Yes, but I need help now.

Visitor: Now you are on the receiving end instead of the giving end. It's hard for you, isn't it?

Patient: Yes.

Right from the beginning, the patient explains her situation. She has had three surgeries; that is a lot to go through. When we hear someone describe a serious experience like that, we need to really take it in and ask ourselves "What would I feel like after having three operations?" It is also interesting to note that the visitor did not verbalize her own beliefs during the visit. Instead, she asked questions in such a way that allowed the patient to voice her reality: protecting the spouse, faith, hope, sadness, changes in lifestyle and feeling like a burden.

Finishing Business

To know that your death is imminent is a gift, even though there may be pain involved. When people die suddenly, they have no opportunity to say goodbye to anyone.

Usually there are at least five things every dying person wants to hear:

"Thank you."

"Please forgive me."

"I forgive you."

"I love you."

and "Goodbye."

Each person can convey these sentiments in his or her own way. For some, they might come up within a single conversation, as that may be the only chance to convey them.

When we have a conversation like this, it is good to remember that we want to keep things on the positive side. Dying people may mention past situations in which they may have made a mistake, or done something to us that they regret. This is their way of apologizing to us. Do not stop them and say, "That's okay, I forgot all about that." Let them say what they have to say. Simply listen. If it is appropriate, when they finish expressing what they need to express, we can say, "I forgive you for that."

We should not bring up negative memories. We want to celebrate the lives of those who are dying and talk about their virtues and positive accomplishments. We want them to feel satisfied with their lives and help them to die free from guilt or negative feelings. Reminding people of their good qualities at the time of sickness and dying is like watering or nurturing a plant. We want to help their hearts to blossom. Otherwise the negative aspect of the mind could suffocate them, bringing up feelings of depression, sadness and regret.

Mother Teresa tells a story that reveals the importance of forgiveness in the process of dying. "We have been created to love and be loved. A young man was dying, but for three or four days fought to prolong his life. The Sister asked him, 'Why do you continue this fight?' 'I cannot die without asking forgiveness from my father,' he answered. When his father arrived, the youth embraced him and asked forgiveness. Two hours later, the young man passed away peacefully."

After a friend of mine's great-aunt died, she narrated her experience:

"I was very close to my aunt, but hadn't seen her for years because she lived on a farm in Africa and I lived in the United States. My aunt was suffering from emphysema after decades of heavy smoking. I wrote to her and mentioned in the letter that every time I heard a dove coo I was reminded of her and of some of the happiest memories of my childhood, because there were so many cooing doves on my aunt's farm.

Many months later, I was sitting in my apartment when I heard a sound at the window—it was the sound of a dove cooing and wings flapping very fast. I went to the window and gently pushed the blind aside. A dove was hovering just inches from the window, flapping its wings to stay in position. I was surprised because I couldn't remember ever having seen any doves in the area around the building. A little while later, the phone rang with the message that my aunt had just died.

"I was deeply distressed, but three days later I had a dream that made me feel at peace. We were somewhere out in the countryside, on a little sand road amongst beautiful green fields and leafy trees. I was standing on the road and my aunt was in the back seat of a car that was beginning to drive away. I told my aunt that I loved her. As the car moved away, my aunt looked at me through the back window and mouthed the words, 'I love you.'"

Though you may not be able to be with someone at the time of their death, a dream like this one could signify the person coming to tell you goodbye in the only way they can.

Having an Agenda

The more attached we are to our loved one, the bigger our agenda will be. For example: We are driving to the hospital after having had a previous visit with our sister who is admitted there. On the way we think, "Gee, it was stuffy in that room! I'm going to open the blinds and windows. Maybe light some incense. I have this nice classical music I am going to put on. I'm going to read to her from scripture and maybe I'll give her a foot massage. I'll bring some beautiful chrysanthemums."

These are all very wonderful ideas, but maybe we fail to realize that because of treatments our sister is very sensitive to light and smell. She prefers the Beatles and Led Zeppelin to classical music. She is allergic to chrysanthemums, and she would love to read *People Magazine* because she feels completely isolated and out of touch with what is going on in the world. Therefore, we always need to ask, ask, ask what she or he would like.

Generally, the more familiar we are with the patient, the less often we will think to ask. We somehow feel freer to impose our preferences on our loved ones. We must remember that the person who is dying now has very little control in her life—we want to empower her with as many choices and as much freedom as possible. If she feels aggravated by us, she cannot walk away.

The simple fact that the patient is forced to be in bed creates a circumstance in which the patient is at the mercy of others. When we walk into a room and, without asking, do things we assume the patient wants, we are rendering her powerless. We are adding to her feelings of helplessness and lack of control.

While taking care of my father, I experienced many instances of having an agenda. He was diagnosed with fourth-stage inoperable lung cancer at the age of forty-nine. As his tumor rested on a nerve, he was taking incredibly strong pain medication. It seemed to me that almost daily he needed to increase his dosage. This was very troubling for me because he had a history of addiction, and I was afraid he was becoming addicted to these pain medicines.

Looking back, although I wasn't aware of it at the time, I was also afraid of losing the person I knew as my father. His sharp intelligence, his wit, and his sunny disposition were becoming muddled, and gradually I was losing the personality to which I was so attached. I was not ready to let him go.

One day, two months into being his caretaker, he asked for his medicine and I thought, "Instead of three tablets of morphine, I'll give him two tablets of morphine and one Vitamin C." When I brought him the tablets, he immediately saw what I had done. He looked at me, saying, "What are you doing? Do you think I want to take this much medicine?" We both started to cry.

This story illustrates how we can be blinded by our attachments. Anytime we have the thought, "I know what's best," or we think we're doing something that is best for the patient, we need to carefully examine our motives. This act on my part was very selfish because I could not accept the changes that were happening so quickly; I wasn't ready to lose my father.

Ideally, try to have a conversation with the patient at the outset of the diagnosis, that addresses questions such as, "How can we help to keep you most comfortable?" or "How much alone time do you need?" Pay close attention to their preferences and habits; are they surrounded by books or are they constantly talking on the phone? Also, throughout the process, clearly and directly ask the patient what they want.

Many people of all faiths believe it is very important to think of God or guru at the time of death. If your loved one has faith or is a devotee, ask them exactly what they want, especially at the time of death. How could they most easily be reminded of God? What is their daily practice or meditation?

Do's and Don'ts

We should always try our best not to say things like, "Don't worry, it will all be okay," or, "There is always a silver lining."

I once found myself in the emergency room in the middle of the night. There had been a three-car accident involving many children. A family of four boys had just watched their mother die. She had been thrown through the windshield. I was comforting the eleven-year-old, just hugging him while he cried. At one point I said to him, "It will be okay." He pulled back from me, and looked me in the eye and said, "No, it won't." After a pause I said, "You're right, it might never feel okay again."

It took an eleven-year-old child to teach me not to say something so bland, thoughtless and untrue. If someone says to you, "I am scared," and you honestly don't know what to say, and if it's true for you, be honest and say, "I am scared too." Answering in such an honest way creates a connection.

It is usually best not to give advice. However, if our loved one is dealing with an important decision concerning their health and treatment, and if they are lucid and capable of making their own decisions, it is important to discuss different scenarios with them.

For example, the patient could say to us, "I'm exhausted. I've been doing this for two years. The cancer has come back. I don't know if I can handle anymore. My doctor wants me to do another round of chemo." We can respond, "It sounds like you need to make a difficult decision. In your life, in the past, when you've had to make very difficult decisions, how did you do it?" If the person says, "I prayed about it and I sat quietly with it for a long time." or "I talked it over with my best friend," we can encourage them to do that in this case. In this way we come to a solution together; we don't just tell someone what to do.

Making a Connection

"Children, this compassion that you feel for the suffering—that in itself will bring them peace; and it will expand your hearts as well. We need to feel empathy with those who suffer."

—*Amma*

You might be called to help a dying person with whom you have little in common. Your brother or sister, or even your mother or father, whom you may have grown apart from, could suddenly get diagnosed with a terminal illness.

I visited one woman, Diane, who desperately needed a liver transplant. She was a recovering heroin addict, and as soon as I started speaking with her, she burst into tears. She was devastated because she had to give away her cats. They carried too many germs and with her weakened immune system, she could not be exposed to germs in her house. To be honest, I struggled to be very patient, because she spoke only of these cats for close to an hour. But as I listened to her, I came to find out that her grandparents, whom she adored and who had raised her, had owned cats. For her cats symbolized love. She had no one else in her life to love, just cats, so this was heartbreaking for her.

I visited a Vietnam veteran named Roy who was into NASCAR (Car Racing) and rode a Harley Davidson. His only form of socializing was playing poker once a month with some friends. I had absolutely nothing in common with this man. I have never attended an auto race and, to be honest, he frightened me. But I noticed that he never had any visitors and this pushed me to continue to knock on his door. I wanted to serve him, so I had to try to find a way to connect with him.

After a couple of visits, during which I learned these things about him, I went to the volunteer resource center in the hospital and got a couple of issues of *Popular Mechanics*, some car-racing magazines, and a pack of playing cards. On my next visit, I gave him the magazines and we played poker. In this case, it was the best way for me to make a connection and bring him some comfort. Sometimes we have to expand our definition of what is spiritual. Bringing someone scripture or religious music may not be the most suitable solution for them. We are there to comfort that person, not ourselves.

Again, Amma exemplifies this quality perfectly. She meets everyone where they are in their particular walk of life. When She meets with students, She becomes a student, relating to them at their level and never dismissing their concerns or questions. The same is true for Indians, Westerners, householders, monastics, children, professionals or the homeless. Amma effortlessly and spontaneously builds bridges, making people feel that She is their own and that She understands them regardless of language or cultural differences.

Signs

Sometimes those who are dying will give us signs or symbols. For instance, they may say, "I had a dream last night. I was packing for a trip, but I couldn't find my passport." This could be a sign that they are trying to tell us they are getting ready to go. They may not even be aware of this on a conscious level. We may ask, "What do you think this dream means?" which in turn could open a whole dialogue that the person wanted to have about death, but did not know how.

Elisabeth Kübler-Ross says, "It is important that we learn the symbolic language many of our patients use when they are unable to cope with their turmoil and are not yet ready to speak openly about death and dying. Sometimes they will use hidden language when they are unsure of the response of their environment, or when they elicit more fear and anxiety on the part of the family members than they experience themselves."[4]

We cannot assume there is going to be a next time.

Once I went to visit a patient named José. He was a Latino man who was suffering from AIDS, leukemia, and cirrhosis of the liver. We had had three or four other visits together, and we had a nice connection.

Even though he was in the intensive-care unit, when I arrived, he was sitting up, eating, and talking with a friend. Because he had a visitor, I did not stay long. When I got to the door to leave, he said, 'I love

[4] Ross., page 17

you.' As we were only acquaintances, this seemed a bit unusual. I just turned and smiled and left. He died that night.

In retrospect I realized he was trying to say goodbye to me. I should have walked back into the room, gone to the side of the bed, taken his hand, and said, "I love you, too. Goodbye." This was really my loss. I missed out on being there for this beautiful, expressive person, and now I will never get the chance again. Do not take your next visit for granted.

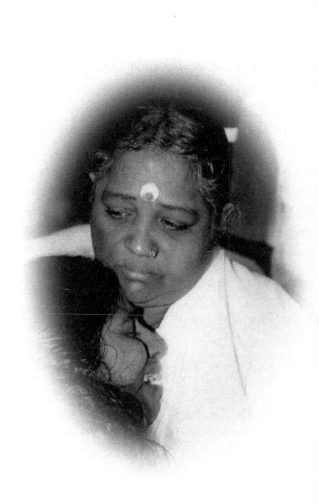

Death

"Death is an art to learn and practice. It can only be practiced if you drop your ego. It can only be learned by practicing meditation. Only when we realize the inevitability of our own death, will we feel an urgency to seek inner peace and true happiness."

—Amma

The Dying Process

"If you die while in a state of deep meditation, it would be such a death that you would not take birth again. Meditation will save us from all kinds of agitation. One need not be a believer in God to do meditation. One can imagine that one is merging in the Infinite just as a river merges with the ocean. This method will certainly help one escape from being agitated."

—*Amma*

When a person enters the final stages of the dying process, two different dynamics are at work. Physically, the body begins the final experience of shutting down, the culmination of which is the cessation of all functioning in the physical systems. The other dynamic of the dying process takes place on the emotional-spiritual-mental plane as the spirit of the dying person begins the final process of release from the body and its immediate environment.

"Actively dying" is a term used to describe the state of those who have entered the process of dying. This is usually a period anywhere from one or two weeks before the death until the actual time of death. Generally, it means patients have stopped eating and drinking. There is sometimes a palpable feeling that they are withdrawing into themselves. Some may lose interest in newspapers and TV. They may no longer have a desire to leave home or even their room. Their attention turns inward as they focus their energy on dying, on separating from this world. They may go in and out of consciousness. Emotionally, a dying person may gradually withdraw from friends and acquaintances until only a small circle of people remains.

Some common themes may appear during this time: an increase in sleeping time, changes in circulation, changes in breathing, less need for food and drink, feeling cold or feverish, restlessness or agitation. There also may be a burst of energy before death; the dying person may become more alert and say things or eat things that they had most recently not been able to.

At this time we, as a visitor, can do a lot to maintain a peaceful atmosphere around them. Our loved ones may talk less as death approaches. Remember to use touch. As words lose their importance, a gentle touch can reassure a dying person that they are cared for and loved.

If the person has many relatives and friends, or if, for example, some long-lost ex-husband shows up, there can be a lot of commotion. Unfortunately, when someone becomes ill, the people who are present do not become saints overnight. In fact, often times negative personality traits become exaggerated. If relationships between family members were already fragile, they often become strained even further. In stress, people succumb to pettiness and jealousy and often act unconsciously.

If a situation arises in which there are loud discussions or even arguments in the room, and the patient is awake, we could ask, "Is this atmosphere okay for you? Would you be happier if we came in one at a time and spent time with you? What would be most relaxing for you?" Again, we should not take over and send everyone out of the room; ask the dying person what he or she wants.

Sometimes we have to become advocates for a person who is unconscious by gently but firmly asking family members, "Do you think you can hold this discussion outside?"

Research shows that unconscious people often can still hear what is going on around them. Thus, we should only talk about positive things. If the person is unconscious, one way to be with them is to sit quietly beside the bed and simply match your breathing with theirs. When he or she inhales, you inhale; when they exhale, you exhale, etc. This is usually a peaceful and calming experience for us as visitors and connects us with our loved one.

Sometimes we need to become advocates for patients when dealing with their family or even with hospital staff. We may feel uncomfortable speaking or asking questions to doctors, nurses or the patient's mother or father. Do not be aggressive, but if someone's behavior seems unsupportive, it is a good idea to investigate.

Some years ago, a friend of mine, Kate, went to visit her uncle at the hospital. He had undergone a severe stroke. He had previously experienced a few light strokes and suffered from epilepsy, so the family had employed a caretaker. The caretaker was in the room when Kate entered. Her uncle could no longer speak or move, but he was clearly affected by her visit. Tears welled up in his eyes. They had not seen each other in a long time. Kate wanted to just be there with him in a loving way, but after a few minutes, even though it was still within visiting hours, the caretaker told her to leave, saying that her uncle was tired and should not see any visitors. My friend instinctively felt this was incorrect, but she obediently left the room.

Two days later her uncle died. She felt a deep sense of regret that she had not stayed with him longer. She did not get the chance to say goodbye or to connect with him on a deeper level. She felt that the woman had asked her to leave because she wanted to control the situation. In retrospect, she felt that she should have insisted on staying.

Another common occurrence while dying is the experience of a vision. Our dying friend may claim to have spoken to people who have already died or even to have seen a holy person or saint. They might speak of seeing distant places and locations that are also not apparent to us.

These visions could be nature's way of helping the person to detach from this life and preparing them for the upcoming transition. Please do not contradict, explain away, belittle or argue about what the person claims to have seen or heard. Just because we cannot see or hear it does not mean it is not real for them. These visions are normal and common. If they frighten the patient, try to reassure them of this.

Leaving

"Death is a part of life. All of us must face it today or tomorrow. What is important is not how we die, but how we live. God has given us the freedom to laugh and cry. Even if we are surrounded by darkness on all sides, we must be able to keep the light within aflame. Just because our loved ones have died, doesn't mean we should always grieve. Our scriptures refer to death as a step into a new life."

—Amma

If we are present when someone actually leaves the body, we can do some things to help their spirit leave or move on. We never want to grab hold of the person and say something like, "Don't leave me!" If possible, we can softly and very gently place our hand on the top of the person's head and speak in a pleasant, calm, and reassuring way.

Over the course of one year, I frequently visited a family with twins. One of the twins, James, was diagnosed with a brain tumor when he was one year old. This family spent a year in the hospital. I became very close to them.

One day the social worker on the floor told me that James would probably die at any moment. The staff brought the other twin in and took pictures of the two of them together. He stayed and played for about an hour and then left. The room was full of friends and family. And so we passed the day like this.

After eleven hours, his breathing became very labored. Every breath he took was painful for all of us to listen to. I started to wonder why James was still holding on. I hypothesized that, maybe, being a two-year-old child, he was afraid to go to a new place and needed his mother's permission and reassurance. Because I was very close to his mother, I felt I could offer a suggestion. I whispered in her ear, "Susan, I think you need to talk him through this. I think he is a little afraid, and I think he really needs your permission to go."

This incredibly courageous woman, without shedding a tear, picked up her two-year-old and said to him, "Baby, it's time to go. You've fought so hard and we love you. John [the twin brother] will be fine. Grandpa is waiting for you. I love you, and I want you to go." He died twenty minutes later.

Sometimes the opposite occurs and a person just does not want to let the loved one go. My friend told the following story:

"I was visiting an acquaintance who was very ill. Her son was having a very difficult time accepting her death. He kept saying, 'Don't leave me!' The other family members and friends were so stressed out by him that I invited him to come outside with me. I stayed with him for quite awhile, letting him cry and talk but also helping him to understand the stress he was creating for his mother. He understood that he needed to give her permission to go, as everyone else had, but he really did not want to do it. We went back inside, and he told her he would be all right but that he was going to miss her very much. She passed within minutes, but he never stopped crying. He shook when he told her to go. It took everything he had."

Sometimes we think we have given permission or that the person knows that we love them and that we are going to be fine. But usually the patient needs to hear it; sometimes more than once. Speaking openly and intimately can be very hard if we are not used to this level of intimacy, or to verbalizing our feelings, but we need to find the courage to express ourselves at that time for our loved one's sake.

Many dying people—be they old or young, men or women—are concerned about those they will leave behind. Some are concerned about financial issues, some emotional. Alex, the eighteen-year-old girl who was desperately in need of a lung transplant was extremely worried about the effect her illness was having on her mother. She was even contemplating suicide because she thought her mother could not endure any more pain. For almost every dying person, the anxiety felt over the loved ones who will be left behind is a huge concern.

Respecting Cultural Differences

With regard to respecting cultural differences, Amma is a great example for all of us. She continuously engages with people of various cultures and races yet, She gives everyone the same attention and love, seeing no difference between anyone.

You might become part of the dying process of someone who has a completely different belief system than your own. We need to honor and respect the beliefs of the dying, even if they include things we consider to be cultural mythologies or superstitions. After one of my Irish friends died, I opened the window because there is a belief among some

Irish that the spirit goes out the window. It was not my belief, but as it was his, I honored it, for because that was his belief, perhaps it was his experience.

Different cultures deal with death in different ways. A friend was telling me that she would never cry in front of a loved one who was dying. She came from a family who believed in the "stiff upper lip" approach and felt that crying would make the patient feel sad. Some cultures choose to protect the patient by not telling them that they are terminally ill and are close to death. We need to honor the different ways in which people deal with such serious situations as death or fatal illness without imposing our belief system onto them.

You may enter a room with emotionally expressive people who are wailing and pounding their chests, or you may go into a room with people who are not touching or talking or crying; they may not even be sitting anywhere near the dying person. Remember that one culture's norms and practices are not better or worse than another's. It is important to respect everyone's cultural behavior and traditions.

Here is a dialogue that I had with a woman who was Greek Orthodox, a religion I knew almost nothing about. Zoi was born in Greece and immigrated to the United States. She had previously spoken to me at length about her religion, culture, food, and the festivals, which were a big part of her life.

Dialogue No. 6 - Cultural and Religious Differences

Patient: I have some bad news. The doctors have found nine tumors in my brain.

Visitor: *[Visitor reaches out and touches her leg and sympathetically looks at her in the eyes.]* I'm so sorry, Zoi. What are you feeling?

Patient: I think I feel shocked. The doctor said that I will have radiation. But first I will go home and talk things over with my family.

Visitor: How will that be for you?

Patient: I'm really worried. The lung and the liver okay, but this brain thing... I'm really worried. I'm not afraid to die. Everybody has to die, but my son. He is so close to me. I try to tell him, "Look, if something happens to me..." But he says, "No, Momma, don't talk like that," and he leaves the room.

Visitor: It sounds like then you are left alone to deal with all of your feelings.

Patient: He is so attached to me—too close. He is too close. I don't know what I am going to do. [*She is so focused on him that she cannot even respond to the statement about not having any support.*]

Visitor: Is telling your son the hardest part of this illness for you right now?

137

Patient: Yes, it is. He will come visit me later. I just don't understand why this is happening to me. I'm a good person. You can ask anyone. Can you tell me why this is happening to me?

Visitor: No, I can't say why. We don't know. Only God knows. I think it's one of life's mysteries. Can you tell me about your relationship with God?

Patient: Last night was not so good. I told God, "I'm sorry, but I have lost my faith."

Visitor: Well, if you were talking to God, you couldn't have totally lost your faith.

Patient: *[Laughs]* I guess you are right. But I'm so angry.

Visitor: That's okay. You can be angry.

Patient: I just don't understand why. *[With great intensity and with raised voice]* Why? Why is this happening?

Visitor: *[Visitor touches her leg and gazes at her with love.]* This must be a very hard and confusing time for you, Zoi.

This conversation is fairly typical when someone first gets a very negative prognosis. There are many issues here: her faith, the always present question, "Why?" and her son who cannot stand the thought of losing his mother. Even though we as caretakers might not share the same belief systems or may come from different cultures, we can stay and listen to the issues that are arising for the patient during the visit.

Children

If the patient has children in his or her life, it is important to include them. It is important to talk to them about what they might be experiencing and to share what we are experiencing also.

Generally speaking, children between the ages of five to ten do not have the vocabulary or ability to fully articulate their feelings. Even more than adults, they need a supportive and safe environment where they can express themselves. Children also need closure. What a child imagines is usually far worse than what is actually happening to a person who is dying.

In some countries such as the United States, a whole new industry has emerged in most major medical centers named Child Life Services. It is a welcomed addition to any medical facility. The people who work there are trained to speak to children according to their development, age and intellectual capacity.

If you are in a situation that involves a child, inquire about this service. If the hospital you are visiting is small or does not have a department of this kind, call a larger medical center close by and talk to them about your situation.

A friend of mine shared this story:

"While working as a chaplain, one night I was called to a 'code blue' and when I arrived, many people were already in the room with the man whose heart had stopped. His wife was standing outside the door, looking in with great anxiety while shielding her six-year-old daughter from seeing what was happening. Nevertheless, the girl could hear it, and felt the heightened energy and stress in the atmosphere.

When the nurse saw me, she immediately called me over and said to the woman, 'This is the chaplain.' I asked her, 'Do you want to be inside with your husband?' She said, 'Yes, but my daughter…' I knelt down and asked the little girl, 'If your mom goes in to help your dad, do you want to stay here with me?' With wide, frightened eyes, she nodded yes. I opened my arms and she ran right into them. I picked her up and walked with her down the hall. First I asked her what her name was and told her mine. Then I said, 'Boy, this must be really scary for you.' 'Yes, it is!' she said. She was nodding her head vigorously in great relief to have someone acknowledge her feelings. I continued, 'If I were you, I'd be scared too.'

We continued to talk until I was told that her father had been successfully resuscitated and we could bring her into the room to see her dad.

During our conversation I simply asked questions to draw her out so that she could express her feelings about her father being hospitalized and the feelings she was having in that very moment. Even if they don't fully understand what is going on, children can pick up the intense energy in such situations.

Somehow, when I opened my arms and she chose to trust me, a safe haven was created. This safe haven needs to be created for children again and again in order for them to release their suffering, fear and pain."

Care Giving for the Caregiver

Sometimes it is not the dying patient but the primary caregiver who needs our care and attention. Caregivers are often afraid to leave the bedside of their spouse or parent, and may become completely exhausted. Serving the caregiver is also very important. You can offer a cup of tea, water or food, or offer to stay with the patient while he or she takes a break.

If we find ourselves called to serve as a primary caretaker, and it looks like we will be in it for the long haul—a month, three months, six months, or a year—we need to think about what we need in order to be able to show up and be present day in and day out.

This kind of service can be both emotionally and physically tiring. After only one hour with a patient we may feel as if we have just gotten off a roller coaster. We may have been laughing, crying and helping them sort through their complicated and constantly changing emotions. They may at one minute want to die and the next, express how difficult it is to let go of people in their life.

This diversity of emotion can take place all in one visit, so it is good to be prepared: What helps you deal with stress? Who can you call when you need a break? It is very difficult to be present and make good decisions when we are exhausted, stressed and over-caffeinated.

Importance of Humor

"Laughter is good for our hearts...Seriousness is a disease, and we should try to leave it and allow ourselves to laugh more. Laughter is good for the health. Laughing... from our hearts is the best way to open up."

—*Amma*

When my father was hospitalized with lung cancer, the priest came to administer the Sacrament of the Sick. That day there were about twenty people visiting him. We were all gathered around his bed and the atmosphere was very solemn; people were crying.

The priest did the anointing, and when he finished my father opened his eyes, and winked at the priest and said, "Good job, Father!"

We all burst into giggles. His humor cut through all the tension in the room. Now we were crying with laughter! It was such a gift to us from my dad and something that he would typically do—make us all laugh.

I am not advocating that it is appropriate to deflect our emotions by making jokes. Many people visiting the sick feel uncomfortable with the feelings that they are experiencing and make jokes out of nervousness to cut the tension. This is not a good idea. We can laugh at their jokes, but we don't want to be sarcastic just because it is a defense mechanism for us.

If laughing does healthfully help to release tension, we might instead suggest watching a funny movie or reading aloud a humorous book by the patient's favorite comedian. A good rule of thumb when being humorous is: be kind, be gentle and be skillful.

Comforting the Grieving

Sometimes we will be of service by comforting the loved ones left behind. If someone has died suddenly, during surgery or in an accident, or even unexpectedly during a long terminal illness, it is best to be more of a silent presence while comforting a grieving friend or spouse. I read a story once about a man who lost his son. When he was asked what he needed, he replied that he just wanted someone to sit beside him on the bench. Sometimes there are no words to say.

I visited a couple who, just moments before, had lost their two-week-old son. He had gotten a fever and was gone in twenty-four hours. They were in shock. The mother kept telling me, "I have to take him home." Their grief was monumental. I was with them for two hours, and I don't think I said more than a few words the entire time. Nothing could be said to alleviate their immense grief. I held them, hugged them and gave them water. What can be said in a situation like that?

There Is No Death

Occasionally when someone is told that because of an illness, they don't have long to live, a transformation can take place; the patient may then be able to see through the illusion of a promise of a better future. When that feeling, "I'm at the end of the line," occurs and there is nowhere else to go—there is the possibility of a shift in consciousness or a tremendous opening of the heart.

I was with my friend Sara for one year, the last year of her life. She was forty years old and diagnosed with leukemia. We spent a lot of time together through the ups and downs of her various treatments. I was even with her during two bone-marrow transplants. We spoke very deeply about spiritual matters even though she described herself as a 'card-carrying atheist.'

Sara had a very powerful presence. The other patients on the floor were always seeking her out for comfort or conversation. Every time she would receive bad news from her doctor, she would say, "Well, let's see what's around the next corner." We meditated together often. Sometimes she would listen to a CD on treating cancer through visualizations, and I would rub her feet.

One day, about a month before she died, after listening to the CD, she started to cry. I thought to myself, "Oh, good, she is finally accepting her mortality."

Up until then, I had found it hard to break through her incredibly positive outlook and talk about the fact that there was a good chance that she would not make it.

I went up close to her and asked if she knew where her tears were coming from. After a while she smiled and said, "I am so full of life. There are no more barriers anymore between you and me, or me and anyone or anything. I only feel love for everything. I am crying because I want everyone to feel this and they can't." She sobbed for a long time, not out of self-pity or fear of death, but out of love and gratitude. She was having a full-blown spiritual experience.

At the time of her death, her husband asked her if she wanted more morphine. She hesitated, and he said to her, "You know, you don't have to keep this up any longer." She smiled and said, "Okay." She died ten minutes later, sitting up, smiling, while looking out a huge picture window.

Dying can be a celebration of life. I was once visiting a Portuguese family. The wife had just given birth. A couple of days before the delivery she learned that her child would not live for long. Her husband, parents and a Catholic priest, who was my friend, were all there. As soon as the nurses brought the baby in, all of the family members starting clapping and cheering and they thrust a camera into my hands and said, "Take pictures!" They all took turns holding him and talking to him in English and Portuguese. "We love you so much." "You are perfect. Oh, you are so beautiful..." The priest and I alternately took pictures and wiped the tears from our eyes.

After about twenty minutes, I was sitting next to the mother, who was holding the baby, and she just turned to me and said, "He is cold. He is turning blue." He then died in her arms.

I was so blessed to be a part of this beautiful, full life, which lasted twenty minutes. These people loved this baby for the full twenty minutes of his life, more deeply and affectionately than some people experience throughout their entire childhood. What a beautiful lesson they taught me. It was an incredibly touching experience for my friend and me; we had never witnessed anything like it.

Many prophets and sages have told us repeatedly in different ways that there is no such thing as death. I have heard death described as leaving one room and entering another, or laying down an old coat that you no longer need. Amma often says, "Death is like the period mark at the end of a sentence. There is small gap, and then we begin writing again."

A friend of mine found out that Arthur, one of her mother's closest friends, was dying of a brain tumor. The doctors told him he had six months to a year to live. About two months later, my friend had a dream. In the dream, Arthur appeared to her. He looked slightly younger and he was not wearing his usual glasses. There was a great sense of peace about him. He said, "Tell your mother that I have died, but I am not dead." The next morning she phoned her mother, who told her that Arthur had died during the night.

Death is an intrinsic part of life. We should not allow it to devastate us. Rather, we can learn from it. During my time as a chaplain, I observed that people with faith or spiritual understanding immensely benefited from the grounding and reassurance it provided them. Riding the train home at the end of each day, after having witnessed so much suffering, I was often overcome with gratitude for Amma's presence in my life. We are so blessed to have Amma's love and compassion to support and soothe us as we face life's challenges. Taking inspiration from Amma's example, may we grow in service and may we grow in compassion.

Amma's Words on Death

"Children, who can run away from death? When you are born, death also comes with you. Each moment of your life you are getting closer to death. People are not aware of this. They are so enmeshed in pleasures of the world that they totally forget this. There is no time when death does not exist. In fact, we lie always between the jaws of death. The wise ones are aware of the inevitability of death and try to transcend it.

"While living 'in life,' a wise person acquires the mental and spiritual strength to live also 'in death' or to live in eternity beyond death. He dies to his ego. Once one dies to the ego, there is no person, and thus there is no one to die. Such people are so full with life that they do not know death. Having transcended death, they know only life, ever-pulsating life everywhere. They become the very essence of life. Death is an unknown phenomenon; it does not exist for them. The death that we know about—the perishing of the body—might happen to them, but that death is only a change for them. They do not fear death of the body. But in life and through death they will remain as the essence of life which will assume another form if they so wish.

"The waves are nothing but the water. After one wave rises and falls, the same ocean waters take the form of another wave in another place. Whatever form or shape they may take, they are nothing but the ocean waters. In a similar manner, the body of a perfected soul may also die like the body of an ordinary human being. The difference is that while a mortal human being considers himself a separate entity—a part, different from the Supreme Consciousness like a single wave isolated from the ocean—a perfected soul is fully aware of his oneness with the Absolute. He knows he is not an isolated wave but the ocean itself, even if he has taken human form. Therefore, he does not have any fear of death. He knows that it is a natural phenomenon, only a change. He knows very clearly that just as a wave rises up, dies away and rises up again in another shape at another place, the body too must pass through birth, death and birth again. *Mahatmas* know that they are the ocean, not the wave. They are the *Atman* [the Self], not the body. But an ordinary person thinks that he is the body, an isolated wave, and that he is finished forever when the body dies. This fills him with fear because he does not want to die. Thus he grieves when he thinks of death. He wants to run away from death."[5]

"Birth and death are only relative. They are not real from the ultimate viewpoint. Like any experience in life, they are two events that a person is bound to go through ... Because of their intensity, nature had devised a method by which man completely forgets these two major moments of his life. It is difficult for an ordinary person to remain aware during his own birth and death. Birth and death are two stages of life in which one is utterly helpless. While in the womb and while emerging out of the womb, the child is helpless. It is the same with a dying person. During both these experiences the ego has receded so far into the background, that it is powerless. Children, you are not aware of what is happening to you during or

[5] Swami Amritaswarupananda. *Awaken Children IV.* Kerala, India: Mata Amritanandamayi Mission Trust, 1992, 270-271.

after death. You have to be fearless and fully aware to be open to the experience. If you are afraid you will be closed to the experience. Only those who have enough depth, who are fearless, and who are constantly in a state of awareness, a state of absolute wakefulness, are able to consciously experience the bliss of death.

"Of course, if you have the capacity to remain conscious and alert while passing through the experience of death, it becomes an ordinary experience like other experiences. Then birth and death do not bother you; you simply smile during both occasions. Death is then no longer a strange experience to you. However, this is possible only if you are at one with your True Self.

"As a result of the realization that you are not the body, but the Supreme Consciousness, the whole center of your existence will be shifted to the Self. You will wake up and realize that you were sleeping, and that the dream which is this world, and all the experiences associated with it, are only a play. You will laugh as you look at this exquisite play of consciousness."[6]

[6] Swami Amritaswarupananda, *Awaken Children VIII*, 164-165.

Practical Application

"*Consoling a miserable soul, wiping the tears of a crying person is greater than any worldly achievement.*"

—*Amma*

I invite you to keep a journal while you are going through this process. Here are some questions that may help you along the way. There are no right or wrong answers; the purpose of these exercises is to help us to grow in awareness.

1. Write down everything you can remember about the visit.

2. At the end of the visit, how did you feel? Refer to the "List of Feeling Words" on the next page.

3. As you recall the visit now, do you have any new or different emotions?

4. What feelings did you hear expressed by the patient? Refer to the "List of Feeling Words" on the next page.

5. What did your non-verbal communication express to the patient?

6. Did anyone enter the room during the visit? How did this change the tone of the visit?

7. Did the patient express any needs? If so, are you or were you able to meet any of those needs?

8. Did you feel uncomfortable at any time? Do you know what caused these feelings?

9. Did you feel prepared going into the visit [i.e. centered, grounded]? If not, what could you do next time to better prepare yourself?

10. Do you feel you emotionally connected with the patient? If not, why not?

11. What will you do differently on your next visit?

12. Did you have an agenda before going in?

13. Did you learn anything about yourself through this experience?

List of Feeling Words

abandoned
abnormal
angry
annoyed
anonymous
anxious
apathetic
at peril
at risk
attached
ashamed
assaulted
awful
awkward
abused
babied
bad
baffled
bamboozled

battle-weary
beaten down
boxed-in
blamed
burdensome
caged
cajoled
callous
calm
cantankerous
capable
captured
careful
cast out
challenged
chaotic
changed
cheated
childlike

choked-up
coerced
combative
complicated
confused
constricted
crucified
crabby
crafty
cranky
crappy
crazed
crazy
crestfallen
crippled
crotchety
cut-off
damaged
damned
dazed
debilitated

deceived
defeated
deformed
defensive
deflated
dependent
deserted
despairing
desperate
despondent
determined
disappointed
difficult
different
disconnected
discontented
discouraged
disempowered
disgusted
doomed
edgy

emasculated
emotional
enraged
excluded
exhausted
expectant
explosive
fearful
flustered
forced
frightened
frustrated
furious
fussy
grateful
grief-stricken
guilty
harassed
hardened
hateful
heartbroken

heavy-hearted
helpless
henpecked
hesitant
hideous
humiliated
hurt
ignored
immobilized
imprisoned
incapable
incapacitated
invisible
isolated
jealous
lackadaisical
left out
lonely
mad
miserable
mistreated

misunderstood
nauseated
negative
neglected
nervous
neurotic
numb
optimistic
ornery
overwhelmed
out of control
outraged
pampered
panicked
patronized
pitiful
positive
powerless
regretful
rejected
rotten

sad
scared
selfish
self-pitying
sensitive
stressed
troubled
vexed
worried

This book is the outcome of a three year collaboration, which came about due to the talent and contribution from the following people: Swamini Krishnamrita Prana, Swami Paramatmananda Puri, Mira, Vineeta, Sachin, Divya, Neeraja, Priyan, Deva Priya, Upasana, Rasya, Haran, Praveena, Kripa Prana, Amala, Kripa, Shubha, Anupama, Hari Sudha, Ramani, Devika, Rajita, Amarthya, Agama, Adam, Atulya, Anavadya, Tarini Ma, Ram Das, Vinaya, Sivani, Chaitanya, Vedavati, Annari and Rod.

I would like to thank every patient and family member I have had the privilege of meeting. Thank you for being my teachers.

100% of the proceeds
from Being with Dying
will go to the charitable projects
of Embracing the World.
For more information, please go to
www.embracingtheworld.org

Book Catalog
By Author

Sri Mata Amritanandamayi Devi
108 Quotes On Faith
108 Quotes On Love
Compassion, The Only Way To Peace:
  Paris Speech
Cultivating Strength And Vitality
Living In Harmony
May Peace And Happiness Prevail:
  Barcelona Speech
May Your Hearts Blossom:
  Chicago Speech
Practice Spiritual Values And Save The
  World: Delhi Speech
The Awakening Of Universal
  Motherhood: Geneva Speech
The Eternal Truth
The Infinite Potential Of Women:
  Jaipur Speech
Understanding And Collaboration
  Between Religions
Unity Is Peace: Interfaith Speech

Swami Amritaswarupananda Puri
Ammachi: A Biography
Awaken Children, Volumes 1-9
From Amma's Heart
Mother Of Sweet Bliss
The Color Of Rainbow

Swami Jnanamritananda Puri
Eternal Wisdom, Volumes 1-2

Swami Paramatmananda Puri
On The Road To Freedom Volumes 1-2
Talks, Volumes 1-6

Swami Purnamritananda Puri
Unforgettable Memories

Swami Ramakrishnananda Puri
Eye Of Wisdom
Racing Along The Razor's Edge
Secret Of Inner Peace
The Blessed Life
The Timeless Path
Ultimate Success

Swamini Krishnamrita Prana
Love Is The Answer
Sacred Journey
The Fragrance Of Pure Love
Torrential Love

M.A. Center Publications
1,000 Names Commentary
Archana Book (Large)
Archana Book (Small)
Being With Amma
Bhagavad Gita
Bhajanamritam, Volumes 1-6
Embracing The World
For My Children
Immortal Light
Lead Us To Purity
Lead Us To The Light
Man And Nature
My First Darshan
Puja: The Process Of Ritualistic
  Worship
Sri Lalitha Trishati Stotram

Amma's Websites

AMRITAPURI—Amma's Home Page
Teachings, Activities, Ashram Life, eServices, Yatra, Blogs and News
http://www.amritapuri.org

AMMA (Mata Amritanandamayi)
About Amma, Meeting Amma, Global Charities, Groups and Activities and Teachings
http://www.amma.org

EMBRACING THE WORLD®
Basic Needs, Emergencies, Environment, Research and News
http://www.embracingtheworld.org

AMRITA UNIVERSITY
About, Admissions, Campuses, Academics, Research, Global and News
http://www.amrita.edu

THE AMMA SHOP—Embracing the World® Books & Gifts Shop
Blog, Books, Complete Body, Home & Gifts, Jewelry, Music and Worship
http://www.theammashop.org

IAM—Integrated Amrita Meditation Technique®
Meditation Taught Free of Charge to the Public, Students, Prisoners and Military
http://www.amma.org/groups/north-america/projects/iam-meditation-classes

AMRITA PUJA
Types and Benefits of Pujas, Brahmasthanam Temple, Astrology Readings, Ordering Pujas
http://www.amritapuja.org

GREENFRIENDS
Growing Plants, Building Sustainable Environments, Education and Community Building
http://www.amma.org/groups/north-america/projects/green-friends

FACEBOOK
This is the Official Facebook Page to Connect with Amma
https://www.facebook.com/MataAmritanandamayi

DONATION PAGE
Please Help Support Amma's Charities Here:
http://www.amma.org/donations

CPSIA information can be obtained
at www.ICGtesting.com
Printed in the USA
BVHW091219130620
581309BV00002B/25